How do I feel about

MY PARENTS' DIVORCE

Julia Cole

Franklin Watts London · Sydney

This edition published in 2001
An Aladdin Book
© Aladdin Books Ltd 1997

Designed and produced by
Aladdin Books Ltd
28 Percy Street
London W1P 0LD

First published in Great Britain
in 1997 by Franklin Watts
96 Leonard Street
London EC2A 4XD

ISBN: 0 7496 2670 4 (hbk)
ISBN: 0 7496 4095 2 (pbk)

A catalogue record for this
book is available from the
British Library.

Printed in the U.A.E.

Designer   Tessa Barwick
Editor   Sarah Levete
Illustrator   Christopher
                O'Neill
Photographer   Roger Vlitos

The author, Julia Cole, is a
trained counsellor and is the
Press Officer for National Relate.
She writes and broadcasts
regularly on relationship issues.

Contents

Introduction

Jon, Anu, Mark and Jade know how it feels when a mum and dad decide to live apart. You may have a friend whose parents are separated or divorced, or your parents may have split up. Join the friends as they talk about their feelings.

My mum and dad are separated. I live with my mum.

I live with my dad and see my mum at weekends.

Jade is my sister. Our parents are getting a divorce.

Even though they're divorcing, we'll still see dad.

JON

ANU

MARK

JADE

What Is Divorce?

Jon is explaining that separation is when two grown-ups who have lived together decide to live apart. If they are married they may also decide to get a divorce. You may hear someone say that his or her parents have split up. This can mean that they are separated or divorced.

Grown-ups can only divorce if they are married. They may separate first.

I don't understand the difference between divorce and separation.

My parents live apart from each other. They are separated.

My parents live apart, too. They've also got a document which says they're no longer married.

Splitting up is when parents separate.

It's also when parents divorce.

▼ Splitting Up

Splitting up is when grown-ups decide to live apart. If they are married, they may decide to divorce. Grown-ups who split up usually live in separate homes. They may live alone or they may live with a new partner.

◀ Who Divorces?

Only grown-ups who have been married can get a divorce, because a divorce is a legal end to a marriage. But grown-ups who are married can still separate without getting a divorce.

Jon, tell us about your parents.

"My parents split up about four years ago. I don't see my dad any more. I live with mum. Because mum and dad never married, they didn't need to get a divorce. I don't think it matters if you call it divorce, separation or splitting up. They all mean that two grown-ups have decided to live separately."

What Happens?

Mark is telling Anu that his dad is going to live somewhere else. When Anu's parents split up, she and her dad moved house. Each situation is different, but most mums and dads want to make sure their children will be OK. Whatever your mum and dad do, you will still be looked after.

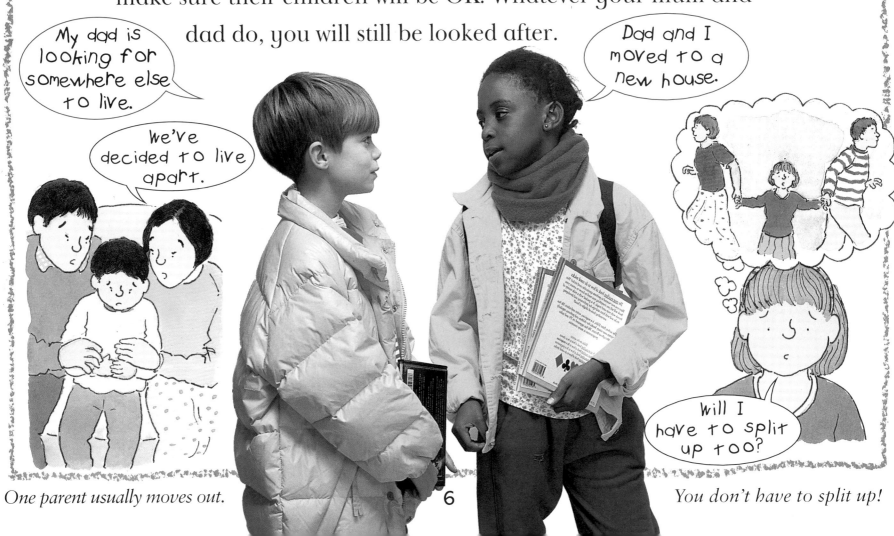

My dad is looking for somewhere else to live.

We've decided to live apart.

Dad and I moved to a new house.

Will I have to split up too?

One parent usually moves out.

6

You don't have to split up!

1. Saba thought divorce or separation happened straight away.

2. Josie thought Saba would forget her. But he wanted to stay friends.

3. Talking helped Josie and Saba to realise that each situation is different.

Why is it different for Saba and Josie?

Saba and Josie now know that every family is different. One parent may move out before you have been told what is happening. Or your parents may tell you that they are splitting up before anything happens. Like Saba you may stay in your home, or like Josie you may have to move house.

1. Sam wanted her mum and dad to stay together, but her mum was moving out.

2. Sam's parents had decided that Sam would stay with her dad.

3. Sam found it difficult to understand how her mum could leave and still love her.

Will Sam's mum still love her?

Sam's mum is going to live apart from Sam and her dad, but this doesn't mean that she will stop loving Sam. She will still see Sam regularly. Some parents stay in contact with their children a lot. Others don't visit very much, but whatever happens, they will always be your mum and dad.

▼ What About Me?

Sometimes your parents will decide between themselves whom you stay with or they may ask you what you think. Sometimes the courts need to help decide this. They may also decide when and if you see your other parent.

Can he live with us in our new house?

◀ Together Again!

The parent from whom you live apart may try to visit or to see you as much as he or she can. However, this may not always be possible. You can ask the parent with whom you live to explain the new situation.

Anu, you live with your dad now. Do you see your mum?

"Yes. When my parents separated they decided that my sister, Isha, and I should live with dad. We moved house and everything. But Isha and I still see mum at weekends and during the holidays."

Why Does It Happen?

Mark is telling Jade why he thinks that their parents are splitting up. There can be lots of reasons why parents split up. They may not love each other in the same way as they used to, or they may meet someone else they want to be with. Whatever the reason, it doesn't mean that they will stop loving you.

▶ *Arguing Again!*

Parents can argue so much they become very unhappy. They may feel that they should part in order to stop the rows. They may decide that even though divorce or separation is upsetting, in the end it will mean that everyone can be happier.

It's quieter here than at home!

▼ *But Dad Loves Her*

Sometimes only one parent wants to live away from the other parent. If this is the case, the parent who doesn't want the other one to leave may find it difficult to accept and understand the new situation.

◀ *New Partners*

One parent may find a new friend they can talk to and get on with better. He or she may choose to live with them instead of your mum or dad. If this happens, you may feel very angry towards your parent's new partner.

1. Jo and Jim Jones were arguing over a computer game.

2. Their mum heard them arguing. She came in and told them off.

3. A week later, Mr and Mrs Jones told Jo and Jim that they were splitting up.

Are Mr and Mrs Jones splitting up because Jo and Jim argued?

No, definitely not. Parents who split up do so because they feel unhappy with each other. Mrs Jones was cross with Jim and Jo, but it had nothing to do with the decision to separate from Mr Jones. It is important to remember that you are not to blame for the separation or divorce of your parents.

Why Does It Happen?

Is it mum's fault for working so hard ...

...or dad's for playing so much golf?

▼ I Don't Understand

Sometimes the situation may be very complicated. If you can, try talking to an older brother, sister or grandparent to help you to understand better what is happening.

It's just that they aren't happy with each other anymore.

◄ Who's To Blame?

You may want to blame one of your parents if they split up. But grown-ups often decide together to separate or divorce. Even if it is just one parent's choice, blaming him or her won't help anyone.

Mark, do you understand why your parents are getting a divorce?

"Jade says it's mum's fault for shouting at dad. But it's not fair to blame mum. Dad shouts at mum, too. I think they are splitting up because they will be happier if they don't live together. I'll miss dad but it will be better if the rows stop."

13

Difficult Feelings

Jade is round at Anu's house after school. She is asking Anu how she felt when her parents split up. Like Jade and Anu, you might have lots of difficult and confusing feelings if your parents separate or get a divorce.

You may feel confused by other people.

You may feel very angry.

▼ Nothing's Changed

After splitting up, one or both of your parents may be sad for a while. This can be hard to understand if they have split up so they would not be upset. It can take time to stop feeling sad.

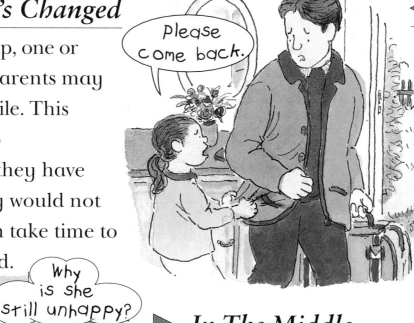

▶ In The Middle

Sometimes you may feel caught in the middle between your mum and dad. If this happens, talk to your parents about it. Why not ask them to talk to each other, instead of saying things to you about the other one?

◀ But I Want Them Both

You may feel upset and want your mum and dad to stay together, even if they have been sad. You may feel angry with the parent with whom you live and want to blame him or her for the situation. These feelings are quite natural.

15

1. Billy was angry that his parents were splitting up. He didn't want them to.

2. At school, Billy wouldn't do what his teacher asked him to do.

3. Billy told his teacher that he felt as if nobody cared about his feelings.

Why did Billy misbehave at school?

Billy was feeling unhappy and angry. He wanted somebody to take notice of his feelings. But Billy didn't have to misbehave in order to get attention. He could have told his parents or his teacher how he felt. It is better to talk about your feelings, rather than getting cross or even getting into trouble.

▼ Why Isn't It OK Now?

Sometimes your mum and dad may argue, even if they don't live together anymore. It can take time for them to sort out how to share the things they used to own together. They may also still feel cross with each other.

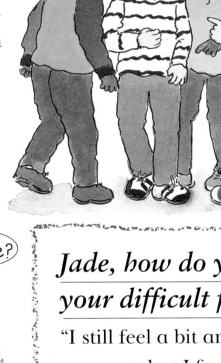

◀ Other People

Sometimes other people don't understand the situation and may say upsetting things about your parents. However hard it is, try to ignore such comments. Instead, chat to good friends and other members of your family.

Why do they still argue?

Jade, how do you cope with your difficult feelings?

"I still feel a bit angry with my mum but I feel better about it now. It was good talking to Anu, even though I know it won't make mum and dad get back together again."

17

Feeling Ok

Getting used to changes in the family is not easy. At first, Anu missed her mum, but she prefers it now because both her parents are happier. Jon took a while to get used to all the changes. He misses seeing his dad, but feels better about things now.

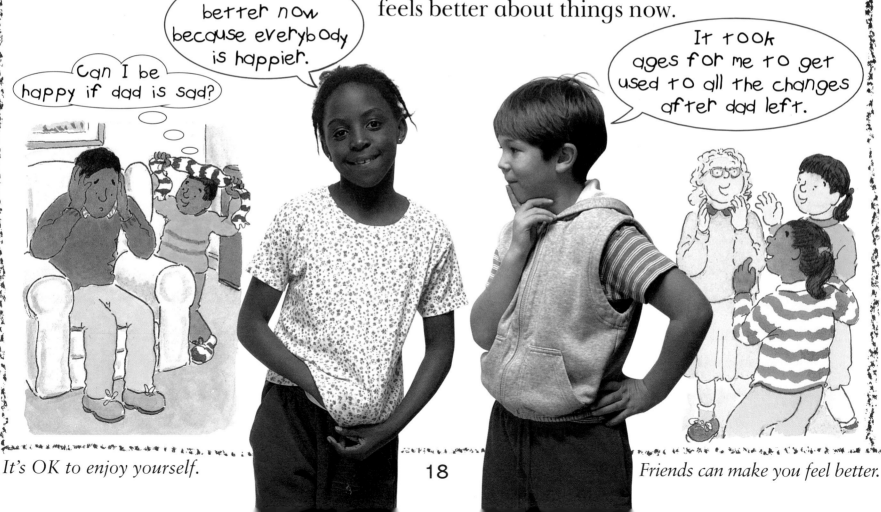

It's better now because everybody is happier.

Can I be happy if dad is sad?

It took ages for me to get used to all the changes after dad left.

▼ In Touch

If you miss your mum or dad, why not write him or her a letter or draw a picture? It may not always be possible to see him or her, but there is nothing wrong in wanting to keep in touch with your other parent.

◀ No Change

Sometimes you have to accept a situation, even though it may not be what you want. If you talk to your parent about your feelings, he or she will be able to understand how you feel about the situation.

▶ Talking Helps

When parents separate or divorce, there will be lots of changes. For instance, you may spend your birthday with only one parent instead of both parents. But just because things are not the same as before doesn't mean that they can't be just as good or even better.

19

1. Lucy's mum and dad had split up. Lucy didn't want to see or talk to her mum.

2. Lucy's dad tried to understand why Lucy was so cross with her mum.

3. Lucy's dad persuaded Lucy to talk to her mum. It made her feel better.

Why did Lucy feel better after she had talked to her mum?

Lucy was upset that her mum had left her dad. Speaking to her mum on the telephone didn't make all of her cross and upset feelings go away, but she was glad she had spoken to her mum. A divorce or separation is upsetting for everyone, but bit by bit, sad feelings do go away as you get used to a new situation.

▼ It's OK To Feel Sad

If your parents split up, you may feel very confused and unhappy. Hiding your feelings can make everything seem even worse. It helps to talk to friends whose parents have also split up or to a close friend whom you trust.

◄ It's OK To Feel Happy

If one or both of your parents are feeling sad you may think that you shouldn't enjoy yourself. It may take a while for your parents to feel OK again, but that doesn't mean that they don't want you to have fun.

Anu, what helped you to to feel OK?

"When mum and dad separated, I felt lonely so I told my best friend at school. When I felt unhappy, she and my other friend cheered me up. It helped, too, to keep doing the things I always did before, like playing in the hockey team."

21

Don't Forget . . .

Jade, what is your advice to someone whose parents are splitting up?

"Talk to your parents about your angry or sad feelings, and any other feelings, too! Then your mum and dad will understand better how you feel. Talk to teachers and friends, too. It's not easy, but you do begin to feel better after a while."

Mark, do you agree with Jade?

"Yes, but also don't forget how your parents feel. They don't want to make you sad. Mums and dads have to sort out what is right for them and for you, even if that means that you may all feel upset for a while. If your parents do separate or get a divorce, they are still your mum and dad. Nothing can change that."

Anu, did it take you long to feel better?

"Quite a long time. Sometimes I still miss seeing my mum every day, but it's much better now because there is no more shouting. I think it helps to keep doing the things that you usually do, like playing with friends or visiting your favourite places."

Jon, how do you feel about not seeing your dad?

"It was really hard at first, but I'm not going to let it stop me from having a good time, because that wouldn't help mum either. I quite like it now, with just me and mum. And lots of friends, too!"

Index